What Did We Do?
Before Computers

by Shannon Berg

FOCUS READERS.

BEACON

www.focusreaders.com

Focus Readers is distributed by North Star Editions:
sales@northstareditions.com | 888-417-0195

Produced for Focus Readers by Red Line Editorial.

Photographs ©: Everett Historical/Shutterstock Images, cover (left), 1 (left); Ollyy/Shutterstock Images, cover (right), 1 (right); Everett Collection/Shutterstock Images, 4; Ryan J. Thompson/ Shutterstock Images, 6; GWImages/Shutterstock Images, 8; Red Line Editorial, 11; thyme/iStockphoto, 13; Suntezza/Shutterstock Images, 15; Gorodenkoff/Shutterstock Images, 16; nathan4847/ iStockphoto, 18; CSU Archives/Everett Collection/Newscom, 21; Rawpixel.com/Shutterstock Images, 22–23; Tinxi/Shutterstock Images, 24, 29; peampath2812/Shutterstock Images, 27

Library of Congress Cataloging-in-Publication Data
Library of Congress Cataloging-in-Publication Data is available on the Library of Congress website.

ISBN
978-1-64493-042-7 (hardcover)
978-1-64493-121-9 (paperback)
978-1-64493-279-7 (ebook pdf)
978-1-64493-200-1 (hosted ebook)

Printed in the United States of America
Mankato, MN
012020

About the Author

Shannon Berg is a young adult novelist, short story and nonfiction author, and poet. Shannon lives in Minnesota with her husband, two children, dog, and cat. Most of her spare time is spent working her way through the stack of books waiting to be read on her nightstand.

Table of Contents

Chapter 1

Homework in 1959

The year was 1959. Patty was doing her homework. She had to write a report about a famous writer. Like students today, Patty went to a library. But there were no computers to help her do research.

 Libraries have always been great places to help students do research.

 Writing notes by hand often helps people remember information.

Instead, Patty used the library's **card catalog**. She found two books about her favorite writer. Patty read both books. She also took notes.

She wrote the important facts in her notebook. Then she went back to her classroom.

There, Patty got more paper from her desk. She used her notes to write the report by hand. Using her pencil, she filled three sheets of paper. Then she gave the papers to her teacher.

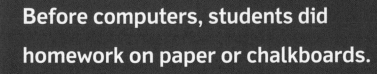

Fun Fact

Before computers, students did homework on paper or chalkboards.

Chapter 2

Organizing Information

Computers make it easy to find information. People in the past used other tools instead. Like today, they could read books at a library. But now, computers make finding resources much easier.

 Before computers, libraries used cards to track when books were due.

Most libraries use computers to track their books. People can type to search for what they want. Before, people had to look by hand. They used a card catalog.

In this system, a large shelf with many drawers holds small paper cards. Each card lists details about

Fun Fact

Melvil Dewey invented the Dewey Decimal System in the 1870s. It helps libraries organize their books.

DEWEY DECIMAL CATEGORIES

Many libraries use the Dewey Decimal System.
It sorts books into groups by subject.

one book. It has the title, author, and call number. People use this number to find the book on the library's shelves.

Today, people use computers to store photos and **documents**. One computer can hold thousands of files. In the past, people had other ways to store information.

Before computers, people were more likely to keep printed copies of important information. All this paper could take up a lot of space.

To store some documents, people made microfiche. These are sheets of very small photos. The photos show pages of newspaper stories or

 A microfiche reader makes tiny pictures large enough to read.

other text. Each photo is very tiny.

The text is too small to read.

To solve this problem, people put

the sheets into a microfiche reader.

This machine makes the photos look bigger. That way, people can read the stories. They look through the pages one at a time.

With computers, people can use **spreadsheets** to track or organize information. These **programs** are especially useful for working with numbers. For example, they help

Fun Fact

Some people still use microfiche readers to read copies of old documents.

 A ledger has lines where people can write
amounts and payments.

banks and people keep track of
money. Before computers, people
had to use paper instead. They
often used books called ledgers.
People wrote all the numbers by
hand. And they did the math on
their own.

$$3)B_{l+\ell}^{m} \quad [l+1] \Big]\, R_1^{m} - \text{independent}$$

$$\cdots A_{l+\ell} \qquad A^{m} H_{\ell}$$

$$\cdots R_l^{m} + \frac{B_{l+3}^{m}}{A_m \,\beta_m} \,\tilde{B} \Big]$$

$$\cdots \big] R_l^{m} + \cdots$$

OK

$$B$$

$$\sum R$$

$$\cdots \Big] R_l^{m} - \text{TRUE}$$

$$\cdots \Big[\frac{B_m}{A(A^{+}} \quad \frac{B}{1} \Big] - \text{FALSE}$$

$$Y - \Big[\frac{X_{l+q}}{A_m A} \quad \frac{Y_m}{A_m A} \Big]$$

$$\cdots [l+1] \Big] R^{m}$$

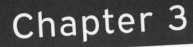

Chapter 3

Work and Writing

Computers can do math very fast. Before computers, people did more math by hand. This method can take a long time. **Calculators** help with some steps. Even so, hard problems can take hours to solve.

Writing one math problem by hand can require an entire chalkboard.

> Early cash registers had buttons or levers that workers used to enter prices.

Computers also help stores track their items. Before, workers had to count the items. This took time. And sometimes they made mistakes.

Stores have to track money, too. At first, workers had to calculate what customers paid. They wrote the numbers on paper. Later, cash registers helped them add. But until the 1970s, workers still had to put in the price for each item.

In most stores today, computers do all this **automatically**. Workers just have to scan items. Prices and totals appear on a screen.

Fun Fact

At first, the word *computer* meant a person who did math.

Writing also took longer before computers. For years, people wrote everything by hand. By the 1920s, many were using typewriters. These machines stamped letters onto paper. But it was hard to go back and fix mistakes.

Later, some typewriters could make changes. They used a special tape to remove ink from the paper. By the 1970s, some typewriters had small **memory cards**. These cards could remember a few pages of

 The Magnetic Card Selectric Typewriter used a memory card to record and retype letters.

typing. A typewriter could redo the letters in this section on its own. Users just had to type the part they wanted to change.

Typewriters

Typewriters were invented in the 1860s. Users slide a sheet of paper into the top of the typewriter. A part called the carriage holds the paper.

Users press the typewriter's keys. Each key connects to a metal letter. When users press a key, the letter hits a ribbon of ink. It makes a mark on the page behind it.

After each letter, the carriage moves. That way, the letters will not overlap. Eventually, the carriage reaches the edge of the page. Next, users slide the carriage back over. Then they can begin the next line.

Early typewriters were often made of mostly metal parts.

Find inspiration in each small thing you encounter each day.
Take a new route home, get lost, and open yourself up for the unknown.

Chapter 4

Computers and Changes

The first digital computers were made in the 1940s. These early computers were very large. Just one computer could take up a whole room. By the late 1970s, computers were smaller and faster.

 Personal computers started to become common in the 1980s.

They were also easier to use. People began buying computers to use at home.

People could easily type and save their writing. They could fix mistakes before printing the pages. In the 1990s, websites and **search engines** made finding information easier, too.

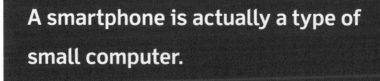

Fun Fact

A smartphone is actually a type of small computer.

 Tablets and laptops let people use computers on the go.

Today, computers do many tasks. Some solve **complex** math problems. Others store huge amounts of information. Stores and libraries use computers to track their items. Computers do many tasks automatically. They make life easier in many ways.

Before Computers

Write your answers on a separate piece of paper.

1. Write a paragraph summarizing the main idea of Chapter 4.

2. Would you rather write using a typewriter or a computer? Why?

3. Which machine lets people look at old newspapers?
    - **A.** a typewriter
    - **B.** a card catalog
    - **C.** a microfiche reader

4. Why might finding information without a computer have taken longer?
    - **A.** People could not find books at the library without computers.
    - **B.** People had no way to know where the library kept each book.
    - **C.** People had to check one book or page at a time.

5. What does **calculate** mean in this book?

*At first, workers had to **calculate** what customers paid. They wrote the numbers on paper.*

    A. to make a sneaky plan
    B. to add or subtract numbers
    C. to type numbers on a computer

6. What does **tasks** mean in this book?

*Today, computers do many **tasks**. Some solve complex math problems. Others store huge amounts of information.*

    A. jobs or activities
    B. names for people
    C. types of food

Answer key on page 32.

Glossary

automatically
Done on its own, without any outside control.

calculators
Electronic devices used for doing math problems.

card catalog
A set of many paper cards listing all the items available from a library.

complex
Very long or hard to solve.

documents
Records of something, such as images, film, or writing.

memory cards
Small objects that store information for a device.

programs
Sets of instructions that tell computers how to perform actions.

search engines
Computer programs that help users find websites or information about a particular topic.

spreadsheets
Documents that use grids to track, organize, and calculate numbers.

To Learn More

BOOKS

Harris, Duchess, with Rebecca Rowell. *Hidden Heroes: The Human Computers of NASA.* Minneapolis: Abdo Publishing, 2019.

Oxlade, Chris. *The History of Computers.* Chicago: Capstone Press, 2018.

Smibert, Angie. *Inventing the Personal Computer.* Mankato, MN: The Child's World, 2016.

NOTE TO EDUCATORS

Visit **www.focusreaders.com** to find lesson plans, activities, links, and other resources related to this title.

Index

C
card catalog, 6, 10–11

D
documents, 12, 14

H
homework, 5, 7

L
ledgers, 15
libraries, 5–6, 9–11, 27

M
math, 15, 17, 19, 27
microfiche, 12–14

S
search engines, 26
spreadsheets, 14
stores, 18–19, 27

T
typewriters, 20–21, 22

W
websites, 26
writing, 5, 7, 20, 26